ALL ABOUT REINDEER

KRISTEN RAJCZAK NELSON

PowerKiDS press

NEW YORK

Published in 2020 by The Rosen Publishing Group, Inc.
29 East 21st Street, New York, NY 10010

First Edition

Editor: Kristen Nelson
Book Design: Reann Nye

Photo Credits: Cover Victor Maschek/Shutterstock.com; p. 5 ALEXEY GRIGOREV/Shutterstock.com; p. 7 Shchipkova Elena/Shutterstock.com; p. 9 SeM/Universal Images Group/Getty Images; p.11 powerofforever/DigitalVision Vectors/Getty Images; p. 13 Espen Solvik Kristiansen/Shutterstock.com; p. 15 New York Daily News Archive/New York Daily News/Getty Images; p. 17 GraphicaArtis/Archive Photos/Getty Images; p. 19 https://commons.wikimedia.org/wiki/File:Hermey_the_elf_and_Rudolph.jpg; p. 21 Vladimir Melnikov/Shutterstock.com; p. 22 Yuganov Konstantin/Shutterstock.com.

Cataloging-in-Publication Data

Names: Rajczak Nelson, Kristen.
Title: All about reindeer / Kristen Rajczak Nelson.
Description: New York : PowerKids Press, 2020. | Series: It's Christmas! | Includes glossary and index.
Identifiers: ISBN 9781725300804 (pbk.) | ISBN 9781725300828 (library bound) | ISBN 9781725300811 (6pack)
Subjects: LCSH: Reindeer--Juvenile literature.
Classification: LCC QL737.U55 R35 2020 | DDC 599.65'8--dc23

CPSIA Compliance Information: Batch #CSPK19. For Further Information contact Rosen Publishing, New York, New York at 1-800-237-9932.

CONTENTS

UP ON THE HOUSETOP

It's Christmas Eve! What's that on the roof? For almost 200 years, stories about reindeer pulling Santa's sleigh have been a big part of Christmas. Their story is told in songs, movies, and books throughout the Christmas season. But, there's some disagreement about how they became a **symbol** of Christmas!

REINDEER OF THE PAST

Reindeer are a kind of deer often called caribou in North America. They live in places with cold weather such as Greenland, Russia, and Alaska. People have long herded and hunted them for food and fur. In fact, the Sami people of northern Europe have been herding reindeer for thousands of years!

Some people believe Christmas reindeer stories come from winter holidays and **customs** of **ancient** peoples. Others point to **mythology**. Norse stories say the god Thor was pulled by two goats in a flying **chariot**. Reindeer as part of Christmas could be a mix of these ideas!

SANTA

The modern story of Santa and his reindeer likely comes from a **poem** that first came out in the 1820s. "A Visit from St. Nicholas" tells of Santa's arrival with "eight tiny reindeer." It names the reindeer, but two of these have changed. "Donner" and "Blitzen" started out as "Dunder" and "Blixem!"

FROM ALASKA TO BIG BUSINESS

In the mid-1800s, hundreds of reindeer were brought to Alaska from Norway. They were meant to help the Inuit people, who didn't have enough food. Not long after, businessman Carl Lomen thought he could make a lot of money off the reindeer. He wanted to sell reindeer meat and fur!

This business idea failed. But Lomen played a big part in connecting reindeer and Santa. He worked with the store Macy's on a big parade in 1926. They used real reindeer to pull Santa's sleigh! It was supposed to **promote** Lomen's business. Instead it showed Americans a story come to life!

SHOES
SHOES
NEW YORK EYEGLASS CENTER
138
138
OPTOMETRIST
CONTACT LENSES
WISE
SHOES
SKIRTS BLOUSES
PINES 34 St
BRASSIERES UNDERWEAR
MERRY CHRISTMAS

THE NINTH REINDEER

Another story also has much to do with Christmas reindeer: the story that introduced Rudolph! In 1939, the store Montgomery Ward put out a coloring book with a story about Rudolph, the red-nosed reindeer. The store gave the book away to shoppers during the Christmas season. The first year, about 2.4 million people received a copy!

A songwriter decided to write a song based on the story of Rudolph. The most well-known **version** came out in 1949 and was performed by singer Gene Autry. In 1964, the story and song were made into a movie! *Rudolph the Red-Nosed Reindeer* is still shown on TV around Christmastime every year.

MORE REINDEER

While the nine reindeer of the 1949 song are the most popular version of Santa's reindeer, they aren't the only ones! Many other stories over the years have names for Santa's reindeer. L. Frank Baum, who wrote *The Wizard of Oz*, even wrote his own story! His reindeer included Flossie and Glossie.

DO YOU BELIEVE?

Reindeer are **majestic** animals you can probably see at the zoo! But do they really pull Santa's sleigh at Christmastime? With the magic of Christmas and your imagination, anything is possible! So when you think you hear hooves on the roof on Christmas Eve, you can decide what you believe—it could be reindeer!

GLOSSARY

ancient: Coming from a time that was long ago in the past.

chariot: A carriage with two wheels that was pulled by animals such as horses.

custom: An action or way of behaving that is common among the people in a certain group or place.

majestic: Large and very beautiful.

mythology: The myths, or stories, of a certain group.

poem: A piece of writing that may rhyme.

promote: To make people more aware of.

symbol: Something that stands for something else.

version: A form of something that's different from the ones that came before it.

INDEX

WEBSITES

Due to the changing nature of Internet links, PowerKids Press has developed an online list of websites related to the subject of this book. This site is updated regularly. Please use this link to access the list: www.powerkidslinks.com/IC/reindeer